50 German Chocolate Recipes

By: Kelly Johnson

Table of Contents

- Classic German Chocolate Cake
- German Chocolate Brownies
- German Chocolate Cupcakes
- German Chocolate Cookies
- German Chocolate Cheesecake
- German Chocolate Pie
- German Chocolate Fudge
- German Chocolate Truffles
- German Chocolate Layer Bars
- German Chocolate Donuts
- German Chocolate Macarons
- German Chocolate Whoopie Pies
- German Chocolate Cake Pops
- German Chocolate Pancakes
- German Chocolate Ice Cream
- German Chocolate Muffins
- German Chocolate Tart

- German Chocolate Granola Bars
- German Chocolate Mousse
- German Chocolate Bread Pudding
- German Chocolate Cinnamon Rolls
- German Chocolate Banana Bread
- German Chocolate Waffles
- German Chocolate Oatmeal Cookies
- German Chocolate Bark
- German Chocolate Scones
- German Chocolate Lava Cakes
- German Chocolate Soufflé
- German Chocolate Chia Pudding
- German Chocolate Milkshake
- German Chocolate Ice Cream Sandwiches
- German Chocolate Fudge Cake
- German Chocolate Marshmallow Bars
- German Chocolate Caramel Squares
- German Chocolate Tiramisu
- German Chocolate Éclairs

- German Chocolate Cheesecake Brownies
- German Chocolate Pudding
- German Chocolate S'mores
- German Chocolate Cake Roll
- German Chocolate Biscotti
- German Chocolate Tartlets
- German Chocolate Crinkle Cookies
- German Chocolate Rice Krispies Treats
- German Chocolate Croissants
- German Chocolate Poke Cake
- German Chocolate Milk Pie
- German Chocolate Sticky Buns
- German Chocolate Popcorn
- German Chocolate Frosting Dip

Classic German Chocolate Cake
 Ingredients:

- 2 cups all-purpose flour
- 1¾ cups sugar
- ¾ cup unsweetened cocoa powder
- 1½ tsp baking powder
- 1½ tsp baking soda
- 1 tsp salt
- 2 eggs
- 1 cup buttermilk
- ½ cup vegetable oil
- 2 tsp vanilla extract
- 1 cup hot water

Filling/Topping:

- 1 cup evaporated milk
- 1 cup sugar
- 3 egg yolks
- ½ cup unsalted butter
- 1 tsp vanilla
- 1½ cups sweetened shredded coconut

- 1 cup chopped pecans

Instructions:

Mix dry ingredients in one bowl. Whisk wet ingredients in another. Combine and stir in hot water.

Pour into greased pans and bake at 350°F (175°C) for 30–35 minutes.

For the filling, heat milk, sugar, yolks, and butter until thickened, then add vanilla, coconut, and pecans.

Cool cakes, layer with filling, and top generously.

German Chocolate Brownies
Ingredients:

- ½ cup butter
- 1 cup sugar
- 2 eggs
- 1 tsp vanilla
- ⅓ cup cocoa powder
- ½ cup flour
- ¼ tsp salt
- ¼ tsp baking powder

Topping:

- ½ cup evaporated milk
- ½ cup sugar
- 1 egg yolk
- ¼ cup butter
- ½ tsp vanilla
- ¾ cup coconut
- ½ cup chopped pecans

Instructions:
Mix brownie ingredients and bake in a greased pan at 350°F (175°C) for 25–30 minutes.

Cook topping ingredients until thickened, stir in coconut and pecans. Spread topping on cooled brownies.

German Chocolate Cupcakes

Ingredients:

Same as cake recipe above, divided among cupcake liners.

Instructions:

Prepare the batter, fill cupcake liners 2/3 full, and bake at 350°F (175°C) for 18–20 minutes.

Top with traditional coconut-pecan frosting once cooled.

German Chocolate Cookies
 Ingredients:

- 1 cup butter, softened
- 1½ cups sugar
- 2 eggs
- 1 tsp vanilla
- 2 cups flour
- ⅔ cup cocoa powder
- 1 tsp baking soda
- ½ tsp salt

Topping:
Same coconut-pecan topping as above.

Instructions:
Cream butter and sugar, then mix in eggs and vanilla. Combine dry ingredients and add. Scoop onto baking sheets and bake at 350°F (175°C) for 10–12 minutes.
Cool and top with coconut-pecan frosting.

German Chocolate Cheesecake

Crust:

- 1½ cups chocolate cookie crumbs
- ¼ cup melted butter

Filling:

- 3 (8 oz) packages cream cheese
- 1 cup sugar
- 1 tsp vanilla
- 3 eggs
- 1 cup melted German chocolate

Topping:
Coconut-pecan filling as above.

Instructions:
Mix crust ingredients and press into pan. Bake at 325°F (160°C) for 10 minutes.
Beat cream cheese and sugar, add eggs one at a time, then stir in chocolate and vanilla.
Bake for 50–60 minutes. Cool, then spread topping.

German Chocolate Pie

Ingredients:

- 1 unbaked 9-inch pie crust
- 1 cup evaporated milk
- ½ cup sugar
- 2 eggs
- 1½ cups German chocolate, melted
- 1 tsp vanilla
- ½ cup coconut
- ½ cup chopped pecans

Instructions:

Mix all ingredients, pour into crust, and bake at 350°F (175°C) for 35–40 minutes. Cool completely before serving.

German Chocolate Fudge

Ingredients:

- 2 cups sugar
- ¾ cup evaporated milk
- ½ cup butter
- 2 cups chocolate chips
- 1 tsp vanilla
- 1 cup sweetened coconut
- ½ cup chopped pecans

Instructions:

Boil sugar, milk, and butter for 5 minutes. Remove from heat, stir in chocolate chips and vanilla.
Fold in coconut and pecans. Pour into pan and chill until firm.

German Chocolate Truffles

Ingredients:

- 8 oz German chocolate, chopped
- ½ cup heavy cream
- 1 tbsp butter
- ½ tsp vanilla
- ½ cup toasted coconut
- ¼ cup chopped pecans

Instructions:

Heat cream and butter, pour over chocolate and stir until smooth.
Chill until firm, then roll into balls. Roll truffles in coconut and pecans.

German Chocolate Layer Bars
  Ingredients:

- 1½ cups graham cracker crumbs
- ½ cup melted butter
- 1 cup semisweet chocolate chips
- ¾ cup shredded coconut
- ½ cup chopped pecans
- 1 (14 oz) can sweetened condensed milk
- ½ cup German chocolate, chopped

Instructions:
Mix graham crumbs and butter, press into a baking dish.
Layer chocolate chips, coconut, pecans, and chopped chocolate.
Drizzle condensed milk evenly over the top.
Bake at 350°F (175°C) for 25–30 minutes. Cool and cut into bars.

German Chocolate Donuts
Ingredients:

- 1 cup flour
- ¼ cup cocoa powder
- ½ tsp baking soda
- ¼ tsp salt
- ½ cup buttermilk
- ½ cup sugar
- 1 egg
- 2 tbsp melted butter
- 1 tsp vanilla

Topping:
Coconut-pecan frosting

Instructions:
Whisk dry ingredients. In a separate bowl, combine wet ingredients, then mix with dry. Pour into a greased donut pan and bake at 350°F (175°C) for 10–12 minutes. Cool and top with coconut-pecan frosting.

German Chocolate Macarons

Shells:

- 1 cup almond flour
- 1¼ cups powdered sugar
- 3 tbsp cocoa powder
- 3 egg whites
- ¼ cup sugar

Filling:
Coconut-pecan mixture or German chocolate ganache

Instructions:
Sift almond flour, powdered sugar, and cocoa. Whip egg whites and gradually add sugar until stiff peaks form.
Fold dry mix into the meringue. Pipe onto parchment and rest 30 minutes.
Bake at 300°F (150°C) for 15–18 minutes.
Cool and sandwich with filling.

German Chocolate Whoopie Pies

Cakes:

- 2 cups flour
- ½ cup cocoa powder
- 1 tsp baking soda
- ½ tsp salt
- ½ cup butter
- 1 cup sugar
- 1 egg
- 1 tsp vanilla
- 1 cup buttermilk

Filling:
Coconut-pecan frosting

Instructions:
Cream butter and sugar, add egg and vanilla. Mix dry ingredients and alternate with buttermilk.
Scoop onto baking sheets and bake at 350°F (175°C) for 10–12 minutes.
Cool and sandwich with frosting.

German Chocolate Cake Pops
Ingredients:

- Leftover German chocolate cake, crumbled
- ½ cup coconut-pecan frosting
- Chocolate coating
- Toppings: shredded coconut, chopped pecans

Instructions:
Mix cake crumbs with frosting. Form into balls and chill.
Insert sticks and dip in melted chocolate.
Decorate with coconut or pecans. Chill until set.

German Chocolate Pancakes

Ingredients:

- 1 cup flour
- 2 tbsp cocoa powder
- 1 tbsp sugar
- 1 tsp baking powder
- ½ tsp baking soda
- ½ tsp salt
- 1 cup buttermilk
- 1 egg
- 2 tbsp melted butter
- 1 tsp vanilla

Topping:
Coconut-pecan mixture

Instructions:
Mix dry and wet ingredients separately, then combine.
Cook pancakes on a griddle over medium heat.
Top with warm coconut-pecan frosting.

German Chocolate Ice Cream
 Ingredients:

- 2 cups heavy cream
- 1 cup whole milk
- ¾ cup sugar
- 1 tsp vanilla
- 1 cup chopped German chocolate
- ¾ cup coconut
- ½ cup chopped pecans

Instructions:
Heat milk, cream, and sugar until dissolved.
Stir in chopped chocolate and cool.
Churn in ice cream maker.
In final minutes, add coconut and pecans.
Freeze until firm.

German Chocolate Muffins
Ingredients:

- 1½ cups flour
- ½ cup cocoa powder
- 1 tsp baking soda
- ½ tsp salt
- ½ cup sugar
- 1 egg
- 1 cup buttermilk
- ⅓ cup oil
- 1 tsp vanilla
- ½ cup chopped German chocolate

Instructions:
Mix dry ingredients. In another bowl, whisk egg, buttermilk, oil, and vanilla. Combine and fold in chocolate.
Spoon into muffin tins and bake at 350°F (175°C) for 18–20 minutes.

German Chocolate Tart

Crust:

- 1½ cups chocolate cookie crumbs
- ¼ cup melted butter

Filling:

- 6 oz German chocolate, chopped
- ½ cup heavy cream
- 1 tbsp butter
- 1 tsp vanilla

Topping:

- ¾ cup coconut
- ½ cup chopped pecans
- ¼ cup sweetened condensed milk

Instructions:
Mix crumbs and butter, press into a tart pan, and bake at 350°F (175°C) for 8–10 minutes.
Melt chocolate, cream, butter, and vanilla. Pour into cooled crust.
Mix topping and spread over chocolate layer. Chill until set.

German Chocolate Granola Bars
Ingredients:

- 2½ cups rolled oats
- ½ cup chopped pecans
- ½ cup shredded coconut
- ⅓ cup German chocolate, chopped
- ½ cup honey or maple syrup
- ¼ cup almond or peanut butter
- 1 tsp vanilla

Instructions:
Mix dry ingredients. Warm honey and nut butter, stir in vanilla.
Combine with dry mix, press into a lined pan.
Chill 1–2 hours before slicing.

German Chocolate Mousse
Ingredients:

- 6 oz German chocolate
- 1¼ cups heavy cream
- 2 egg yolks
- 1 tbsp sugar
- ½ tsp vanilla
- ½ cup toasted coconut
- ¼ cup chopped pecans

Instructions:
Melt chocolate. Whip 1 cup cream to soft peaks.
Whisk yolks with sugar and ¼ cup heated cream.
Combine with chocolate, fold in whipped cream, vanilla, coconut, and pecans.
Chill 2–3 hours before serving.

German Chocolate Bread Pudding
Ingredients:

- 5 cups cubed bread
- 2 cups milk
- ½ cup cream
- ½ cup sugar
- 2 eggs
- 1 tsp vanilla
- 1 cup chopped German chocolate
- ½ cup shredded coconut
- ½ cup chopped pecans

Instructions:
Whisk milk, cream, eggs, sugar, and vanilla.
Pour over bread in a baking dish.
Fold in chocolate, coconut, and pecans.
Bake at 350°F (175°C) for 35–40 minutes.

German Chocolate Cinnamon Rolls
 Dough:

- Your favorite cinnamon roll dough (homemade or store-bought)

Filling:

- ¾ cup brown sugar
- 2 tsp cinnamon
- 1 tbsp cocoa powder
- ½ cup shredded coconut
- ½ cup chopped pecans
- 2 tbsp butter, softened

Icing:
Coconut-pecan frosting or chocolate glaze

Instructions:
Roll out dough, spread filling, roll up and slice.
Bake at 350°F (175°C) for 20–25 minutes.
Top with warm frosting.

German Chocolate Banana Bread
Ingredients:

- 1½ cups flour
- ½ cup cocoa powder
- 1 tsp baking soda
- ½ tsp salt
- ½ cup butter
- ½ cup sugar
- 2 ripe bananas
- 2 eggs
- 1 tsp vanilla
- ½ cup chopped German chocolate
- ½ cup shredded coconut
- ½ cup chopped pecans

Instructions:
Cream butter and sugar, then mix in bananas, eggs, and vanilla. Add dry ingredients, then fold in chocolate, coconut, and pecans. Pour into loaf pan and bake at 350°F (175°C) for 55–60 minutes.

German Chocolate Waffles

Ingredients:

- 2 cups flour
- ¼ cup cocoa powder
- 2 tbsp sugar
- 1 tbsp baking powder
- ½ tsp salt
- 2 eggs
- 1¾ cups milk
- ⅓ cup melted butter
- 1 tsp vanilla
- ½ cup chopped German chocolate

Instructions:
Mix dry and wet ingredients separately, then combine.
Stir in chocolate.
Cook in a waffle iron.
Top with coconut-pecan syrup or frosting.

German Chocolate Oatmeal Cookies
Ingredients:

- 1 cup butter
- 1 cup brown sugar
- ½ cup sugar
- 2 eggs
- 1 tsp vanilla
- 1½ cups flour
- 2 cups rolled oats
- 1 tsp baking soda
- ½ tsp salt
- 1 cup shredded coconut
- ½ cup chopped pecans
- ½ cup German chocolate, chopped

Instructions:
Cream butter and sugars, add eggs and vanilla.
Mix in dry ingredients and fold in coconut, pecans, and chocolate.
Scoop and bake at 350°F (175°C) for 10–12 minutes.

German Chocolate Bark

Ingredients:

- 12 oz German chocolate, chopped
- ½ cup toasted coconut
- ½ cup chopped pecans

Instructions:

Melt chocolate and spread it onto a parchment-lined baking sheet.
Sprinkle with coconut and pecans.
Let cool at room temperature or refrigerate until set.
Break into pieces.

German Chocolate Scones

Ingredients:

- 2 cups flour
- ¼ cup cocoa powder
- ¼ cup sugar
- 1 tbsp baking powder
- ½ tsp salt
- ½ cup cold butter, cubed
- ½ cup chopped German chocolate
- ½ cup shredded coconut
- ½ cup chopped pecans
- ¾ cup heavy cream
- 1 tsp vanilla

Instructions:
Combine dry ingredients. Cut in butter.
Add chocolate, coconut, and pecans.
Mix in cream and vanilla just until dough forms.
Shape, cut into wedges, and bake at 400°F (200°C) for 15–18 minutes.

German Chocolate Lava Cakes

Ingredients:

- 4 oz German chocolate
- ½ cup butter
- 2 eggs
- 2 egg yolks
- ¼ cup sugar
- 2 tbsp flour
- ½ tsp vanilla

Instructions:

Melt chocolate and butter. Whisk eggs, yolks, sugar, and vanilla.
Combine with chocolate, then fold in flour.
Pour into greased ramekins and bake at 425°F (220°C) for 11–13 minutes.
Serve warm with coconut and pecans.

German Chocolate Soufflé
 Ingredients:

- 4 oz German chocolate
- 3 tbsp butter
- 3 eggs, separated
- 2 tbsp sugar
- ½ tsp vanilla
- Pinch of salt

Instructions:
Melt chocolate and butter. Let cool slightly and stir in yolks and vanilla.
Beat egg whites with salt and sugar until stiff.
Fold into chocolate mixture.
Pour into greased ramekins and bake at 375°F (190°C) for 12–15 minutes.
Top with a coconut-pecan sauce.

German Chocolate Chia Pudding
Ingredients:

- 1¾ cups milk (any type)
- ¼ cup cocoa powder
- ¼ cup maple syrup or honey
- ½ tsp vanilla
- ½ cup chia seeds
- ¼ cup shredded coconut
- ¼ cup chopped pecans
- ¼ cup chopped German chocolate

Instructions:
Whisk milk, cocoa, sweetener, and vanilla.
Stir in chia seeds. Refrigerate overnight.
Top with coconut, pecans, and chocolate before serving.

German Chocolate Milkshake

Ingredients:

- 2 cups chocolate or vanilla ice cream
- ½ cup milk
- ¼ cup coconut
- ¼ cup chopped pecans
- ¼ cup chopped German chocolate
- Whipped cream (optional)

Instructions:
Blend all ingredients until smooth.
Top with whipped cream, coconut, and extra chocolate if desired.

German Chocolate Ice Cream Sandwiches

Cookies:

Use soft German chocolate cookies (see prior cookie recipe).

Filling:

Chocolate or coconut-pecan ice cream

Instructions:

Scoop ice cream between two cookies.

Roll edges in toasted coconut or chopped pecans.

Freeze until firm.

German Chocolate Fudge Cake

Cake:

- 1¾ cups flour
- ¾ cup cocoa powder
- 1½ tsp baking powder
- ½ tsp baking soda
- ½ tsp salt
- 1 cup sugar
- ½ cup brown sugar
- ½ cup oil
- 2 eggs
- 1 tsp vanilla
- 1 cup buttermilk
- ½ cup hot water or coffee

Frosting:
Coconut-pecan filling/frosting

Instructions:
Mix dry ingredients. In another bowl, whisk wet ingredients.
Combine and pour into two greased 8" cake pans.
Bake at 350°F (175°C) for 25–30 minutes.
Cool, layer, and frost.

German Chocolate Marshmallow Bars
Ingredients:

- 1 box German chocolate cake mix
- ½ cup butter, melted
- 1 egg
- 2 cups mini marshmallows
- 1 cup semi-sweet chocolate chips
- ½ cup shredded coconut
- ½ cup chopped pecans

Instructions:
Mix cake mix, melted butter, and egg. Press into a greased 9x13 pan.
Bake at 350°F (175°C) for 10 minutes.
Top with marshmallows, chocolate chips, coconut, and pecans.
Bake another 8–10 minutes. Cool before slicing.

German Chocolate Caramel Squares
Ingredients:

- 1½ cups flour
- ½ cup cocoa powder
- ½ cup brown sugar
- ¾ cup butter, melted
- 1 cup caramel sauce
- ¾ cup shredded coconut
- ½ cup chopped pecans
- ½ cup chopped German chocolate

Instructions:
Mix flour, cocoa, sugar, and butter. Press into pan and bake at 350°F (175°C) for 12–15 minutes.
Spread caramel, sprinkle with coconut, pecans, and chocolate.
Return to oven for 5 minutes. Cool and chill before cutting.

German Chocolate Tiramisu

Ingredients:

- 1 package ladyfingers
- 1 cup brewed coffee, cooled
- 8 oz mascarpone cheese
- 1 cup whipped cream
- ½ cup powdered sugar
- ½ cup shredded coconut
- ½ cup chopped pecans
- ½ cup grated German chocolate

Instructions:
Dip ladyfingers in coffee and layer in dish.
Blend mascarpone, sugar, and whipped cream.
Layer over ladyfingers, then top with coconut, pecans, and chocolate.
Repeat. Chill at least 4 hours before serving.

German Chocolate Éclairs
 Shells:

- Choux pastry (butter, water, flour, eggs)
  Filling:

- Coconut-pecan pastry cream or custard
  Topping:

- Melted German chocolate

Instructions:
Bake éclair shells. Fill with coconut-pecan pastry cream.
Dip tops in melted German chocolate. Chill to set.

German Chocolate Cheesecake Brownies
Brownie Base:

- Your favorite fudge brownie recipe
  Cheesecake Swirl:

- 8 oz cream cheese

- ¼ cup sugar

- 1 egg

- ½ tsp vanilla

- ½ cup shredded coconut

- ¼ cup chopped pecans

Instructions:
Prepare brownie batter and pour into pan.
Whisk cheesecake ingredients and swirl into brownie batter.
Bake at 350°F (175°C) for 30–35 minutes.

German Chocolate Pudding

Ingredients:

- ½ cup sugar
- 3 tbsp cocoa powder
- ¼ cup cornstarch
- 2¾ cups milk
- 1 cup chopped German chocolate
- 1 tsp vanilla
- ½ cup coconut
- ¼ cup chopped pecans

Instructions:
Whisk sugar, cocoa, cornstarch, and milk in a saucepan.
Cook until thick. Stir in chocolate, vanilla, coconut, and pecans.
Chill before serving.

German Chocolate S'mores
 Ingredients:

- Graham crackers
- Toasted marshmallows
- Squares of German chocolate
- Toasted coconut and chopped pecans (optional)

Instructions:
Sandwich chocolate and marshmallows between graham crackers. Add coconut and pecans if desired. Warm briefly to melt.

German Chocolate Cake Roll
Cake:

- Thin chocolate sponge cake (flour, eggs, cocoa, sugar)
  Filling:

- Coconut-pecan frosting

Instructions:
Bake sponge in a jelly roll pan. While warm, roll up with parchment.
Unroll, spread filling, and roll back up.
Chill, dust with powdered sugar or drizzle with chocolate.

German Chocolate Biscotti

Ingredients:

- 2 cups flour
- ½ cup cocoa powder
- 1 tsp baking powder
- ½ tsp salt
- ¾ cup sugar
- 3 eggs
- 1 tsp vanilla
- ½ cup shredded coconut
- ½ cup chopped pecans
- ½ cup chopped German chocolate

Instructions:

Mix dry ingredients. Beat eggs and vanilla, then combine with dry mix.
Fold in coconut, pecans, and chocolate.
Shape into two logs and bake at 350°F (175°C) for 25 minutes.
Cool slightly, slice, and bake slices for 10 minutes on each side until crisp.

German Chocolate Tartlets
Crust:

- Pre-made tart shells or homemade chocolate shortcrust
  Filling:

- 1 cup sweetened condensed milk
- ½ cup shredded coconut
- ½ cup chopped pecans
- ½ tsp vanilla
  Topping:

- Melted German chocolate

Instructions:
Mix filling ingredients and spoon into baked tart shells.
Bake at 350°F (175°C) for 10–12 minutes.
Cool and drizzle with melted chocolate.

German Chocolate Crinkle Cookies
Ingredients:

- 1 cup flour
- ½ cup cocoa powder
- 1 tsp baking powder
- ¼ tsp salt
- ½ cup sugar
- ¼ cup brown sugar
- 2 eggs
- ¼ cup melted German chocolate
- ½ tsp vanilla
- ½ cup shredded coconut
- ¼ cup chopped pecans
- Powdered sugar (for rolling)

Instructions:
Mix dry ingredients. Beat eggs, chocolate, and vanilla; combine with dry mix. Stir in coconut and pecans. Chill dough, then roll into balls and coat with powdered sugar.
Bake at 350°F (175°C) for 10–12 minutes.

German Chocolate Rice Krispies Treats

Ingredients:

- ¼ cup butter
- 4 cups mini marshmallows
- ½ cup chopped German chocolate
- 6 cups Rice Krispies cereal
- ½ cup shredded coconut
- ½ cup chopped pecans

Instructions:

Melt butter and marshmallows in a pot. Stir in chocolate until melted.
Mix in cereal, coconut, and pecans.
Press into a greased pan and cool before slicing.

German Chocolate Croissants

Ingredients:

- Store-bought or homemade puff pastry or croissant dough
- ½ cup shredded coconut
- ½ cup chopped pecans
- ½ cup chopped German chocolate
- 2 tbsp brown sugar

Instructions:

Roll dough into triangles. Sprinkle coconut, pecans, chocolate, and sugar. Roll up and bake at 375°F (190°C) for 12–15 minutes or until golden. Drizzle with melted chocolate if desired.

German Chocolate Poke Cake

Ingredients:

- 1 box German chocolate cake mix (or homemade)
- 1 can sweetened condensed milk
- ½ cup caramel sauce
- 1 cup shredded coconut
- ½ cup chopped pecans
- 1 tub whipped topping
- Chocolate shavings (optional)

Instructions:

Bake cake in a 9x13 pan. While warm, poke holes all over.
Pour condensed milk and caramel over the cake.
Cool completely, then spread whipped topping and sprinkle with coconut, pecans, and chocolate.

German Chocolate Milk Pie
 Ingredients:

- 1 chocolate pie crust
- 1 cup whole milk
- ½ cup sweetened condensed milk
- ¼ cup cocoa powder
- 2 tbsp cornstarch
- ½ tsp vanilla
- ½ cup chopped German chocolate
- ¼ cup shredded coconut
- ¼ cup chopped pecans

Instructions:
Whisk milk, condensed milk, cocoa, and cornstarch over heat until thickened.
Stir in vanilla, chocolate, coconut, and pecans.
Pour into crust, chill until set.

German Chocolate Sticky Buns

Dough:

- Sweet roll dough (homemade or store-bought)

Filling:

- ½ cup brown sugar
- 2 tsp cinnamon
- ½ cup chopped German chocolate
- ½ cup coconut
- ½ cup chopped pecans

Topping:

- ¼ cup butter, melted
- ¼ cup brown sugar

Instructions:

Roll dough, spread filling, and roll into a log. Slice into buns. Place in a pan greased with butter and brown sugar mixture. Let rise, then bake at 350°F (175°C) for 20–25 minutes.

German Chocolate Popcorn
Ingredients:

- 8 cups popped popcorn
- 1 cup chopped German chocolate
- ½ cup shredded coconut
- ½ cup chopped pecans

Instructions:
Melt chocolate and drizzle over popcorn spread on parchment.
Sprinkle with coconut and pecans.
Let cool until chocolate hardens, then break into clusters.

German Chocolate Frosting Dip

Ingredients:

- 8 oz cream cheese, softened
- 1 cup sweetened condensed milk
- ½ cup shredded coconut
- ½ cup chopped pecans
- ½ cup chopped German chocolate
- 1 tsp vanilla

Instructions:
Beat cream cheese and condensed milk.
Fold in remaining ingredients.
Serve with fruit, cookies, or pretzels.

www.ingramcontent.com/pod-product-compliance
Lightning Source LLC
LaVergne TN
LVHW081322060526
838201LV00055B/2406